The Illuminated Lettering KIT

George Thomson

CHRONICLE BOOKS
SAN FRANCISCO

First Published in the United States
in 2004 by Chronicle Books

This book was conceived, designed,
and produced by
THE IVY PRESS LIMITED
The Old Candlemakers, West Street,
Lewes, East Sussex BN7 2NZ, U.K

Creative Director: Peter Bridgewater
Publisher: Sophie Collins
Editorial Director: Steve Luck
Senior Project Editor: Rebecca Saraceno
Design Manager: Tony Seddon
Designer: Andrew Milne
Artwork Assistant: Joanna Clinch
Picture Research: Lynda Marshall

ISBN 0-8118-4488-9
UPC 765165-107075

Distributed in Canada by
Raincost Books
9050 Shaughnessy Street
Vancouver, B.C. V6P 6E5

10 9 8 7 6 5 4 3 2 1

Chronicle Books LLC
85 Second Street
San Francisco, C.A. 94105

www.chroniclebooks.com

Manufactured in China

contents

ABOVE: *A page from* The Lindisfarne Gospels (c. A.D. 698) *showing a page from the beginning of St. Luke's Gospel.*

introduction

THERE ARE FEW OF US WHO DO NOT ADMIRE THE BEAUTY OF AN
ILLUMINATED MANUSCRIPT OR WHO DO NOT RECOGNIZE THE SKILL
OF THE ARTIST WHO PRODUCED IT. *THE LINDISFARNE GOSPELS* AND
BOOK OF KELLS OF THE SEVENTH AND EIGHTH CENTURIES, WITH THEIR
ILLUMINATED PAGES, ARE CONSIDERED TO BE AMONG THE GREATEST
WORKS OF ART THE WORLD HAS SEEN. THE ILLUMINATED MANUSCRIPTS
OF THE MEDIEVAL PERIOD CELEBRATE THE ARTISTRY OF THE SCRIBES
AND THE MONKS OF THE MIDDLE AGES, WHO WERE INSPIRED BY THEIR
RELIGIOUS CONVICTIONS IN JUST THE SAME WAY AS WERE THE
ARCHITECTS WHO DESIGNED THE GREAT CATHEDRALS.

THIS KIT WILL PROVIDE ALL THE INFORMATION AND TECHNIQUES YOU
NEED TO LEARN ABOUT THE WORLD OF ILLUMINATED LETTERING. YOU
WILL DISCOVER HOW TO START WITH A SIMPLE LETTER AND CHANGE IT
INTO SOMETHING MUCH MORE ADVENTUROUS. YOU WILL BE SHOWN
HOW TO ADD DECORATION AND PATTERN TO LETTERING AND HOW TO
USE BOTH COLOR AND GOLD EFFECTIVELY. BY FOLLOWING THE STEP-
BY-STEP PROJECTS, YOU WILL BE ABLE TO MAKE GREETING CARDS,
BOXES, AND OTHER ILLUMINATED ITEMS THAT MAY ENCOURAGE YOU TO
PURSUE YOUR ART TO A HIGHER LEVEL.

PART ONE
the basics

WHAT EXACTLY IS "ILLUMINATION"?
WE COMMONLY APPLY THE TERM TO A
MANUSCRIPT, OR OTHER ARTIFACT,
USUALLY WITH LETTERING THAT IS
RICHLY DECORATED WITH COLORFUL
AND GILDED PATTERNS OR DESIGNS.
STRICTLY SPEAKING, ILLUMINATED
LETTERING IS LETTERING THAT "LIGHTS
UP." THIS EFFECT IS ACHIEVED BY
RAISING THE GOLD SLIGHTLY ABOVE
THE SURFACE OF THE PAGE SO THAT
THE LIGHT CATCHES THE EDGE OF THE
GILDED LETTERS OR SHAPES. THE
TECHNIQUE OF PRODUCING RAISED
GILDING WILL BE DESCRIBED IN THIS
BOOK. HERE WE WILL INTERPRET THE
TERM "ILLUMINATED LETTERING" VERY
LOOSELY AND INCLUDE LETTERING AND
DECORATION THAT INVOLVES THE USE
OF METALLIC MEDIA, INCLUDING
RAISED GILDING, METALLIC PAINTS,
COLOR AND/OR DECORATION.

The pens, brush, ink, and paint supplied with this kit are all you need to get started. Other equipment and media are referred to in the text from time to time so that you can choose, if you wish, to tackle the exercises and projects in a more advanced way. All of the projects on pages 44 to 81 can be successfully completed using the colors and gold paint included with the kit. If you want to extend the choice of colors and perhaps even attempt raised gilding, for which simple directions are given, then materials will be widely available.

Illuminated lettering can be used in many situations, but it is not really practical to apply it to something where you require a large number of copies. For instance, it wouldn't be practical to use it on a greeting card if you were sending it to several hundred people! Illumination works best when used much more sparingly—just a touch of gold here and there. More often, illumination will be used for that very special creation, perhaps a poem or other favorite text for framing.

LEFT: *The initial letter "P" taken from the* Winchester Bible *(c. 1150–1180).*

ABOVE: *An extract from* English School, *Psalm 38 (c. 1380), showing David pointing to his mouth. This medieval manuscript is from the collection of the Earl of Leicester, Holkham Hall, England.*

LEFT: *The letter "lights up" as the light strikes the edge of the raised gold.*

history of illuminated lettering

LEFT: *Although illumination was not used by the Romans, they created interesting letter combinations and "ligatures" like this double "A."*

RIGHT: The Lindisfarne Gospels. *St Jerome's letter to Pope Damascus,* c. A.D. 698 (British Library, London, England).

ROMANS, GREEKS, AND CELTS

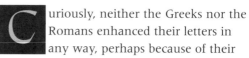

Curiously, neither the Greeks nor the Romans enhanced their letters in any way, perhaps because of their belief in the importance of traditional form and proportions, although sometimes the Romans used ligatures or other lettering combinations for effect. Later, when vellum replaced papyrus as the principal material for important documents (sometime in the fourth century A.D.), an important milestone was heralded: the beginning of the era of the great manuscript books. The *Calendar of 354* by Furius Dionysius is said to have been an illustrated volume (but this has been determined from a copy of a copy as the original no longer survives). The *Vergil Augusteus* in the Vatican Library, also probably fourth century, is the earliest example of a manuscript that uses enlarged initial letters. By the fifth century, monasteries and their associated scriptoria (writing rooms) were established. It is not long afterward that we see the embryos of what we know as illumination: the stems of initial letters being turned into birds or fish.

By the sixth century, the uncial letterform had developed as a book hand (formal, calligraphic-style writing used for large amounts of text). Although its origin is uncertain, it must have developed in some way from one of the Roman scripts. Between the fifth and eighth centuries, we start to see ascenders and descenders, which were already known in the Roman "new cursive." Letterforms became more like our capital and lowercase (small letters) that we use today. The round uncial and half uncial forms were particularly suited to embellishment, and the Celtic scribes who produced the "Insular" manuscripts, including *The Lindisfarne Gospels* and the *Book of Kells*, took full advantage in their great masterpieces of book art. They were also highly creative in inventing new letterforms, possibly influenced by Greek scripts, Ogham, and even Runes. Sometimes these forms were cursive and flowing, sometimes they were geometric.

Decoration was applied to letterforms in several ways. The strokes of letters often finished in the form of animals (usually birds or fish). Letters were sometimes outlined with dots. The strokes of the letters themselves were filled with interwoven patterns or spirals, and less frequently with figurative designs. The counters of letters (space inside), spaces between letters, and background were decorated with flat color, geometric patterns, and sometimes fantastic animals. Gold was used extensively on the richly decorated "incipit" pages, the first pages of each chapter.

ABOVE: *The* Book of Kells. *The page concerns the crucifixion of Christ from the Gospel of Matthew, c. A.D. 800 (Trinity College, Dublin, Ireland).*

The black ink used by the scribes was made from carbon in the form of fine soot or "iron-gall," a compound of sulphate of iron and powdered oak apples. Animal, vegetable, and mineral extracts were used for color pigments. These were bound with gum, egg yolk, or albumen. We do not know the composition of glue to which the gold was applied, but it included such materials as chalk, fish glue, sugar, honey, gelatin, and even oxide of lead.

THE MEDIEVAL MANUSCRIPT

The period between the ninth century and the beginning of the Middle Ages proper (the early twelfth century) was, arguably, one of the most important in the history of lettering. We see the development of the "Carolingian minuscule," which incorporates the final forms of our lowercase letters, and which was to be a major influence on later styles in the Renaissance and the calligraphic revival of the ninteenth and twentieth centuries. From it, the medieval gothic forms evolved. The significance of this period in relation to illumination is more due to the return of the use of classical Roman capitals. To begin with, these followed the Roman traditional form very closely. Gradually a new form developed, the "versal" letter, with its characteristic bulging curves, entasis (narrowing) of the verticals, and very fine serifs. In its extreme form, it became known as the "gothic capital," a term that is misleading as it has little to do with the typically compressed, usually angular medieval gothic script.

Versal and gothic capitals placed great emphasis on the counter shape of the letter and its extended serif, both of which were particularly suited to enhancement. They were the principal building blocks of medieval illuminated manuscripts. The counters of the letters became the location for miniature painting. The decorative elements in the earliest medieval manuscripts tended to be fairly abstract in form, comprising lines and shapes, sometimes in the form of simple foliage. There was, however, an increasing trend toward much more figurative designs in which the plants, flowers, insects, birds, and animals sometimes can be identified. This resulted in a decreased importance of the actual letters.

We tend to think of medieval manuscripts as being strictly of a liturgical nature. However, there were Latin "bestiaries" illustrating real and semimythical creatures and herbals to satisfy the demands of medical science. There were, for example, many illuminated copies of the Greek herbal of Pseudo-Apuleius.

Paper was brought to the West early in the middle ages, but it was not used in quantity until the fifteenth century, when printed books made their appearance. Initially, printed books imitated the handwritten manuscripts, both in lettering style and illumination, and they cost no less. When printing became the main production method for books and documents, the art of illumination declined rapidly and was limited to poor attempts at embellishment in legal and other more formal texts.

13   *History of illuminated lettering*

ABOVE: *The* Nuremberg Chronicle *of 1493 was one of the earliest great printed books. It used illustration rather than illumination, although the initial letters at the beginning of paragraphs still have a manuscript look.*

ILLUMINATION TODAY

With the Renaissance and printing, writing was no longer the sole property of a few skilled scribes. Copybooks introduced the italic script and developments of it to anyone who could afford to buy these handwriting manuals. The illuminated manuscript had virtually disappeared and the functional printing press satisfied the thirst for even more reading matter. Illumination was replaced by illustration, although the copybooks often demonstrated how to draw animals and figures with a writing pen in a calligraphic way. Ultimately, the italic hand was corrupted to a characterless and often illegible "copperplate" script.

In the mid-ninteenth century, William Morris studied Renaissance handwriting. A little later, Edward Johnston studied the Carolingian minuscule. Through them, an appreciation of good letterform, based on sound principles, was fostered and the result of their work is reflected in the quality of calligraphy today. Illumination was promoted through the work and efforts of Graily Hewitt, whose most significant contribution was the rediscovery of the craft of raised and burnished gilding that had been lost for 500 years.

Illuminated work during the twentieth century (particularly in the later half), largely followed the tradition of the medieval manuscript, with decorated and gilded initial letters that were often close replicas of those of more than half a millennium before. However, in the last few decades, illumination has taken a new direction. While it continues to be used in a fairly traditional way, artists such as Dave Wood and Donald Jackson have recently begun to blur the edges between calligraphy and fine art by taking a much less traditional approach to their work, using abstract areas of brilliant color and lettering that is entirely an integral facet of design.

Some calligraphers use lettering as designs and patterns—sometimes legible, sometimes not. We live in an exciting period for calligraphy, lettering, and illumination. A whole range of approaches can be used without fear of being accused of not following a tradition. While one experiment may fail, another will be a triumph. The more adventurous you are with your ideas, the more fun it will be.

LEFT: *The John Frontispiece from Gospel and Acts—the First Volume of The Saint John's **Bible by Donald** Jackson (England). Raised and burnished gold on gesso, powder gold, gouache, and casein color with Chinese stick ink on calfskin vellum. Reproduced by permission of Saint John's University, Minnesota.*

BELOW: *"Ecclesiastes" by Dave Wood (Australia). The gold lettering in the center is decorated with foil that has been cut, folded, and hinged.*

WRITING
INSTRUMENTS
AND MEDIA

The traditional writing tool of the scribe is the quill pen, an instrument made from the wing feather of a goose, turkey, or other bird. The end of the shaft of the feather (the part that attached it to the bird) is trimmed using various cuts to form a square or chisel-shaped tip. This is usually referred to as the broad-edge pen. The important characteristic of the broad-edge pen is that it writes thick and thin strokes and produces the familiar "calligraphic" look. Incidentally, don't be persuaded by what you see in the movies—the "veins" of the feather were stripped from the shaft, otherwise the pen would be difficult to control. Although some calligraphers still advocate the use of a quill pen, most now use metal nibs that are shaped in the same way as the traditional writing instrument. The pen nib has a vertical split that gives it some flexibility and is fitted with a small metal "reservoir" that controls the ink flow.

There are many other types of pen. Indeed, anything that can make a mark can be considered to be a writing instrument, including a piece of wood, felt, or card

ABOVE: *After removal of the veins, the feather is trimmed with a series of cuts to form a broad-edge pen.*

RIGHT: *The small metal reservoir fits below the nib of the pen to control ink flow.*

LEFT: *The pen supplied in this kit. Note the broad-edge shape of the nib, which produces calligraphic thick and thin lines.*

stock, if they are cut to a suitable shape and can hold ink or paint for long enough. Among the more familiar writing tools are poster pens, bamboo pens, automatic pens, fountain pens, and fiber-tip pens. Whatever writing instrument you use, you must consider very carefully what sort of liquid writing media it uses. There are many kinds of ink on the general market as well as more specialized inks you can find at art supply stores. For the very finest calligraphy, the best black ink is nonwaterproof "Indian" ink, but some care is required so that this is not dissolved by the colored inks or paints which you will use for decoration. Colored inks should be used only if the uneven effect they produce is what you want. The most brilliant and permanent colors can be achieved by using artists' watercolor. This is more expensive than "poster" color or gouache, but the results are well worth the money. The inks used in fountain and fiber-tip pens are not suitable for important work, but are good for experiments and rough trials of your designs. The exception to this is the metallic ink fiber-tip pen that can be used for gilding very small areas. Its permanence and brilliance is not as good as more traditional materials and you must be careful that the medium doesn't show on the reverse side of the paper (if this matters).

ABOVE: *A range of writing instruments (top to bottom): technical pen, bamboo pen, automatic pen, fountain pen, fiber-tip pen, and calligraphy pen.*

ABOVE: *The bottle of black ink supplied with the kit. Use this for writing text with the calligraphy pen or for drawing fine black lines with the brush.*

RIGHT: *The watercolor paints supplied with the kit. For illumination, you will usually use these in their pure form, rather than mixed. They can be thinned with clean water.*

drawing and painting equipment

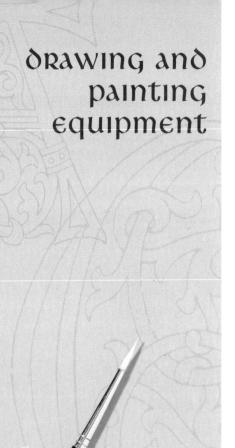

LEFT: *The brush supplied with the kit. Note that it tapers to a fine point.*

*T*here are several essential tools that you need for drawing, decorating, and illuminating lettering. Most of these are supplied with this kit and the others you may have or can buy very cheaply. It is important that suitable pencils, erasers, and brushes are used and we will consider each in turn.

Pencils

Any pencil can be used for sketch ideas, but when you draw up your final design, there are conflicting requirements. The pencil must be hard enough so that it can be sharpened to a good, sharp point but soft enough so that it doesn't indent the paper and can be removed with an eraser afterward. A soft or medium-hard pencil grade is best.

Erasers

So-called plastic erasers are by far the best. They will remove both pencil and other marks and leave your paper undamaged. Avoid rubber erasers.

Brushes

Good brushes are much easier to use and are less likely to deposit hairs on your work than cheap ones. Quality sable brushes, sold in artists' material stores, are best and will last for a long time. In theory, a single medium-size brush, like the one included in this kit,

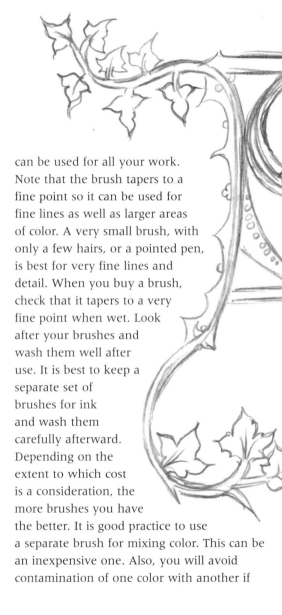

can be used for all your work. Note that the brush tapers to a fine point so it can be used for fine lines as well as larger areas of color. A very small brush, with only a few hairs, or a pointed pen, is best for very fine lines and detail. When you buy a brush, check that it tapers to a very fine point when wet. Look after your brushes and wash them well after use. It is best to keep a separate set of brushes for ink and wash them carefully afterward. Depending on the extent to which cost is a consideration, the more brushes you have the better. It is good practice to use a separate brush for mixing color. This can be an inexpensive one. Also, you will avoid contamination of one color with another if

ABOVE: *A pencil tracing from a medieval illuminated letter.*

you have a different brush for each color. As illuminated lettering tends to involve the use of pure primary colors, this is not as impractical as it might seem.

A sharp pointed pen nib is useful for drawing fine lines. You may find it easier to control than a very fine brush. You don't have to restrict yourself to inks with pen nibs. Artists' watercolor, thinned a little and combined with a tiny amount of gum arabic, will flow as well as ink.

Gold and other metallic media

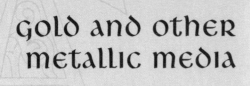

*A*dding a touch of metallic color to your illuminated lettering is sure to attract attention. This will add a shine and sparkle. The term "metallic color" has been used here because you can apply a range of colors other than gold, including silver, blue, green, and even red. Metallic color can be applied in different ways, but you should be aware that the brilliance and permanence of the different forms vary and, unfortunately, the better effects and improved permanence are achieved at greater expense and require greater skill. However, this book will introduce you to some techniques that improve the effectiveness of even the simplest and least expensive materials and produce results of which you will be proud.

Metallic pens

Fiber-tipped pens that write in gold, silver, and other metallic colors are readily available, easy to use, and inexpensive. The brightness of the color they produce is limited but can be improved through burnishing. The problem with some of these pens is that the medium they use to hold the metallic material is absorbed through the writing surface and can spread or discolor the back of the paper. However, they are particularly useful for applying a small amount of metallic color to multiple copies—photocopies, for example—of the same design.

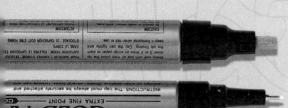

ABOVE: *Metallic fiber-tip pens are great for the quick application of small amounts of gold. Be careful that the solvent they use doesn't bleed through to the other side of your paper.*

Metallic powder

The same metallic material that is used in paint can be obtained separately for you to mix yourself. Combined with gum arabic or a similar binding medium, it produces a water-soluble medium. Gold powder is useful for retouching.

Metallic ink

As metallic ink uses a resin to bind the powder, it presents the same problem of "bleed" as pens. You must shake the bottle very well so that the color can be applied evenly. The brightness of the color is about the same as that achieved with pens.

Metallic paint

Metallic paint can be mixed with water and does not present the problems of "bleed." The color can be less brilliant than ink but can be improved with burnishing.

ABOVE: *The gold paint supplied with the kit is easy to use and can be thinned with water.*

ABOVE: *Real gold leaf is extremely thin and can be difficult to handle. It is also expensive. However, it is the best way to achieve the brightest, smoothest gold.*

Gold leaf

Traditional leaf was made by beating gold by hand to an extremely thin sheet. A piece a few inches square virtually disappears when rubbed between the fingers. It is supplied either between thin sheets of tissue or lightly attached to a protective paper, which makes it easier to handle. The gold is applied to a raised ground of "gesso" or a modern PVA substitute. The burnished gold shines like no other medium. Beware of less expensive gold leaf substitutes—the gold leaf that is used on buildings or by monumental masons. These are very difficult or impossible to apply to a gesso or other ground. Platinum leaf is also available, but is prohibitively expensive and more difficult to use than gold.

paper and other surfaces

BELOW: A selection of different papers: handmade, tinted cartridge and plain cartridge paper, and watercolor.

ellum first made its appearance during the first and second centuries A.D. Real vellum is prepared calfskin. Parchment is made from sheepskin. Before they can be used for writing, they must be treated by rubbing with pounce, made from powdered pumice, so that the surface is smooth and free from grease. Skins are different on each side—the "smooth," whitish side, the preferred side for writing, is the flesh side of the animal while the rougher, yellower side is the hair side. Vellum is preferred by some calligraphers, parchment by others, but both, in their modern forms, are rather stiff and do not compare with that used for medieval manuscripts.

Paper arrived in the West in the early Middle Ages, but was not used in quantity until the fifteenth century. It is a wonderful material and, for all but the purist, paper is the preferred writing surface. It is readily available, inexpensive, easy to write on, relatively stable, and, if a suitable paper is used, will not discolor through time.

When choosing a paper for writing and illumination, several factors should be considered. The surface should be smooth and not too absorbent so that you can write easily on it with a pen. If you are simply sketching ideas, any paper will suffice. For finished work you should always use an acid-free paper, otherwise it will quickly turn yellow or even brown, especially if exposed to light. Colored papers, red in particular, will rapidly fade and you should always consider coloring the background yourself. The thickness of the paper is important if you plan to work on both sides—in the case of a small booklet, for instance. If the paper is too thin, your lettering or designs will show through. Paper that is too thick is difficult to fold.

The best papers for illuminated lettering are acid-free and handmade or moldmade. Several paper companies supply a range of these papers in large sizes and in different thicknesses. They are purchased mainly by watercolor artists and the surface of the majority of them is rough and unsuitable for lettering. However, most suppliers' ranges of moldmade papers include one that has a "hot-pressed" surface which is ideal for illuminated lettering. Always store paper, and your finished work, in a dry atmosphere—any moisture will reduce the lifetime of the paper.

LEFT: *A modern interpretation of a versal "S."*

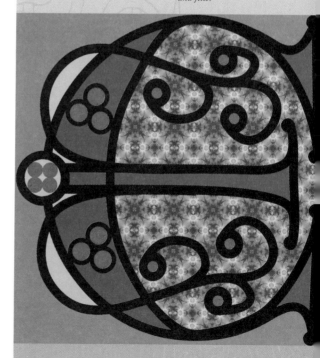

BELOW: *Even computer technology can produce illumination using lines and fills.*

PART TWO
technique

IF YOU WERE ASKED TO DEFINE THE SHAPE OF A LETTER, THE CHANCES ARE THAT YOU WOULD DESCRIBE THE LINEAR FORM. A CAPITAL "B," FOR EXAMPLE, IS A VERTICAL LINE TO WHICH TWO CURVED LINES ARE ATTACHED. WE PROBABLY THINK LIKE THIS BECAUSE OF THE WAY WE LEARNED TO WRITE—WITH A MOVING LINE THAT DESCRIBED THE LETTER. IF WE WANT TO APPRECIATE LETTERFORMS FULLY, WE HAVE TO SEE THEM IN QUITE A DIFFERENT WAY.

RIGHT: *Our appreciation of letterform is greatly enhanced when we learn to see and understand the importance of the counter shapes within and between letters.*

ALPHABETS AND LETTERFORMS

Look at the first word "PEN" in the top illustration below. What do you see? It looks like a set of straight lines and a curve. Look at the same word in the lower illustration. What do you see this time? Now it is a set of shapes, some within and some between the letters. This is what lies behind an understanding of letterform—the important features of lettering are the shapes contained within the letters (the counters) and the shapes between the letters.

We have inherited an alphabet that is wonderfully flexible and that can withstand modification and distortion to a considerable extent. However, it is a code, and to interpret that code we must stick with some basic rules.

line spacing
line spacing

line spacing
line spacing

SPACING

SPACING

One of these rules relates to proportion. Although some type designers have attempted to impose their own proportions on the letters of the alphabet, none has done it successfully. We can go only so far. The letters "O," "M," and "W," for example, are wide letters, while "t," "s," and "f" are narrow. If we make them of equal width, they look odd. In terms of letter proportion, nothing has changed since the days of the Roman inscriptional capitals and Carolingian minuscule "lowercase" letters.

Bad letter spacing can spoil an otherwise good piece of work. When you are writing or drawing lettering, the important thing to remember is that the space between letters should be the "visual" space—that is, the space that looks equal, and not the physical distance between letters. Be especially careful with the lowercase letters "c" and "r," which have very large open counters. Be careful not to space words too widely. The width of the letter "f" between words is usually enough.

Line spacing depends on a number of factors, including the height of the ascender (the line that rises above lowercase letters, in "h" for example), length of the descender (the line that drops below the letter, in "g" for example), and the proportion of the lettering. Round letters with short ascenders and descenders need more space between the lines than narrow letters with long ascenders and descenders. Line spacing also depends on the number of words per line. Text with very few words per line (fewer than eight) or an unusually large number of words (more than fourteen) needs more interlinear space, otherwise legibility is impaired.

letter formation

LEFT: *Drawing an accurate outline before coloring letters or shapes makes it much easier when you come to fill the letters with color.*

BELOW LEFT: *The outlined letter filled with bright color.*

1 t is a fallacy to think that the most important skill required to draw well is manual control of the pencil, pen, or brush. Drawing is seeing. Of course, you have to develop hand–eye coordination to be able to represent what you see, but the lesson here is that it is much more important that you see what you are looking at— form, scale, and proportion. Translating this to paper is secondary.

There are two things that will make drawing letters easier for you. Firstly, work in a well-lit, clean, and uncluttered environment. Secondly, use a good pencil with a lead that is neither too hard nor too soft, and use it very lightly on the paper—you are not attempting to make three-dimensional letters!

Turn the paper regularly so that you are working at the most convenient angle for the lines that you are drawing. Most of the lettering that you will use for illumination will be formal and will comprise smooth straight lines and elegant curves. Try to draw freely and naturally and don't be concerned about making mistakes. Your eraser lets you draw over and over again until you get it right.

Once you have drawn your lettering as a pencil outline, you will probably move on to completing the design, using color applied with a brush or, even, a fine-pointed pen. Use the brush freely and let the hairs of the tool do the job for you. Avoid tentative strokes with the tip of the brush. The more carefully you have drawn your outlines, the easier it will be for you to apply color, gold, or other metallic effects.

Many books have been written on calligraphic technique. Here we can give only some basic principles of good practice. Details of how to write specific calligraphy styles are provided later. Rule guidelines lightly in pencil before you start. Always fill a broad-edge pen from below with a brush to avoid getting ink or paint on the upper surface (see caption below). Write with the pen held so that the angle of the straight edge of the nib stays constant. The angle will depend on the lettering style. Always pull the pen toward you—don't try to push it, as it may catch the paper, or smudge, or the nib may break. When you use a calligraphic pen, try to keep in mind that you are writing, not drawing. Calligraphy should have a rhythm and flow that is quite different from drawn lettering, although the two can easily be combined.

ascender
counter

x-height

descender

xhp

LEFT: *The different parts of letters: the ascender, x-height, counter, and, finally, the descender.*

RIGHT: *The pen should be filled below the nib with a brush to avoid getting ink on the upper surface.*

the Roman alphabet

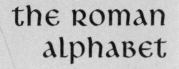

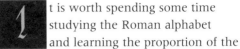

1 t is worth spending some time studying the Roman alphabet and learning the proportion of the letters, the relative widths of the lines, and the forms and scale of the serifs. A thorough understanding of this alphabet will help you to appreciate its variants and the many other lettering styles that derive from it.

It is possible to construct Roman lettering with a calligraphic pen, but for the purposes of illumination the letters are usually drawn. It can help you to learn the letter shapes if you trace them from this or other examples. Photocopied enlargements can make good specimens. Try drawing the letters very large— this will help you see the forms more easily.

Use Roman capitals as single illuminated letters or as decorative initial letters.

ABCDEFG
HIJKLMN
OPQRSTU
VWXYZ

the round, or foundation, hand

1 f you are new to calligraphy, you can't do better than to begin by learning how to write this script. It will develop an understanding of many of the basic principles of using a broad-edge

BELOW: *The x-height of the letters should be about four times the width of the pen nib that you are using, and the ascenders and descenders about three times. You can work this out by drawing little rectangles horizontally with the pen and then marking these off on your paper before ruling guidelines.*

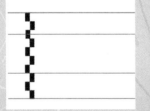

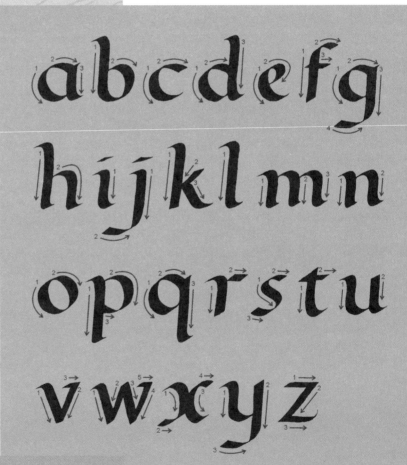

pen, such as keeping a constant pen angle, letter construction, and spacing. Although it can appear to be a very simple, static form, it should be written with some freedom. Have a practice, using the alphabet below.

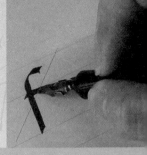

BELOW: *Capitals are best written in a simple form, following Roman capital proportions.*

ABCDEFG
HIJKLMN
OPQRSTU
VWXYZ

ıtalıc

1 talic is a cursive form. It is
fundamentally a handwriting style
and should reflect the free flow of
the pen. However, it can be written in a more
formal manner but should never appear stiff

abcdefg
hijklmn
opqrstu

or constructed. Use your broad-edge pen with a pen-angle of 40–45°. When you write, make sure that you retain the thick and thin strokes that come naturally from keeping the pen angle constant.

Macbeth

RIGHT: *Roman capitals and italic calligraphy go well together. Alternatively, you can write the capitals with the broad-edge pen, simply following the Roman forms. Italic is a good style to use for text. True italic capitals are ideal as subjects for flourished letters, as shown in another section of the book.*

ABCDEFG
HIJKLMN
OPQRSTU
VWXYZ

versals

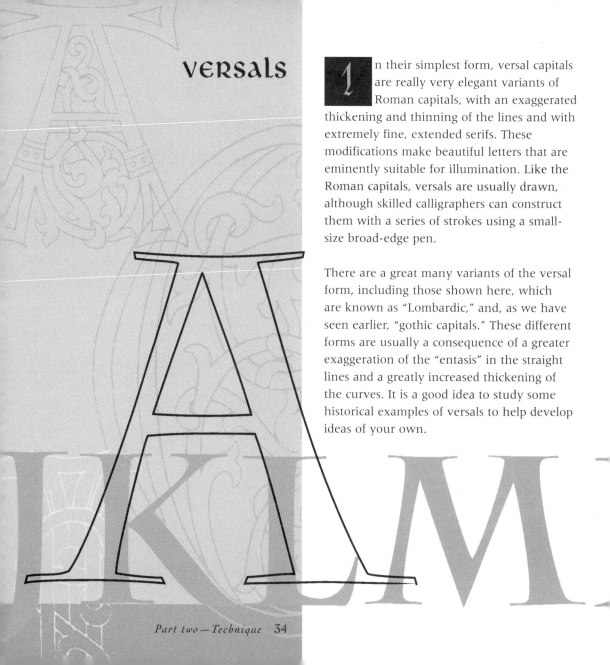

1 n their simplest form, versal capitals are really very elegant variants of Roman capitals, with an exaggerated thickening and thinning of the lines and with extremely fine, extended serifs. These modifications make beautiful letters that are eminently suitable for illumination. Like the Roman capitals, versals are usually drawn, although skilled calligraphers can construct them with a series of strokes using a small-size broad-edge pen.

There are a great many variants of the versal form, including those shown here, which are known as "Lombardic," and, as we have seen earlier, "gothic capitals." These different forms are usually a consequence of a greater exaggeration of the "entasis" in the straight lines and a greatly increased thickening of the curves. It is a good idea to study some historical examples of versals to help develop ideas of your own.

ABCDEFG
HIJKLMN
OPQRSTU
VWXYZ

gothic

Gothic was used almost exclusively in European medieval manuscripts. The lettering is made up from a series of angular lines. It is rather narrow in proportion and heavy in weight. All of these characteristics make the gothic lettering a

BELOW: *There are many different forms of Gothic lettering, some far less angular and some not so narrow in proportion. Take a look at illustrations of medieval manuscripts and spot these variations.*

abcdeefg
hijklmn
opqrstu
vwxyz

highly textural style. Indeed, a variant of it is called "Textura." When used for text, gothic lettering is written with a broad-edge pen, but it is not the easiest form to write well. Large capitals can be fun to draw, flourish, and illuminate.

A B C D E F G

H I J K L M N

O P Q R S T U

V W X Y Z

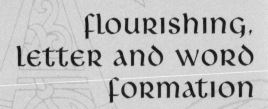

flourishing, letter and word formation

C alligraphers often add flourishes to letters to add interest to the forms, to help create more interesting combinations of forms, or to help fill out a line. Illumination develops the technique further by using more elaborate flourishes to "decorate" letters and to create shapes for color, pattern, and even illustration. Before we explore ways to do this, we will explore the effects of modifying letterform and applying flourishes.

We have seen the importance of the counter and interletter spaces. The basic forms of these should be left unaffected by flourishes or decoration. Take an extreme and simplistic example: The capital "B" comprises two counter shapes, rather like two capital "D"s. We can extend part of the letter without it affecting its legibility. If a third counter shape is added and the same part of the letter is flourished, we no longer recognize it as a "B." Of course, you wouldn't apply such extreme modifications to letters, but the same principle applies when more subtle changes are made. Try changing the round "bowls" of letters such as "B," "C," "D," "G," and "O" to rectangles and see the effect on legibility.

Retaining a sound basic form when flourishes and decoration are applied to lettering is even more important when more than one letter is

ABOVE: *Adding shapes to a letter without consideration of its basic form can result in unsightly distortion and loss of legibility.*

LEFT: *Flourishes should grow from the letter and respect the original form.*

MINIMUM

ABOVE: *In some lettering styles, words written all in capitals are almost illegible—gothic capitals, for example.*

involved. Illuminated capitals are, almost by definition, initial letters that are not intended to be used to make complete words. Flourished gothic capitals, for example, become illegible when used as complete words. It is possible to flourish and decorate complete words, but you must be much more restrained with what you plan to do. It is often better to apply the effect on only the first letter or to use a minimal amount of decoration throughout the word.

While illumination usually involves the use of color, it can also be in black and white, in which case basic letter shapes or words can be distinguished from the decoration by using heavier (i.e., thicker) lines. The use of color can help greatly to resolve problems of legibility if, for instance, a letter or word is picked out in one single, fairly dominant color and the illumination uses other colors.

ABOVE: *Letters of similar color or tone to the decoration are difficult to read.*

LEFT: *Color can be used to make an illuminated letter more legible.*

BELOW: *Letters can be made much clearer if their weight is greater than the decoration.*

"decorating" letters

LEFT: *Letters can be enhanced by the addition of decorative elements such as flourishes. Here a very restrained floral pattern is added to the serif.*

Before you embark on illumination, you should ask why you are doing it. Whatever the reason, you should choose a style of decoration or enhancement that is appropriate for the job in hand. A medieval style will not be suitable for a teenage birthday card, for example, where a more contemporary approach would be appropriate.

There are three approaches to illumination. One is to decorate the lines that form the letters, another is to enhance flourishes, and a third is to leave the lettering untouched and illuminate adjacent parts of the design. Of course, these approaches can be combined in the same layout. Irrespective of the approach you take, always start with the basic letterform, not the decoration, and let the illumination grow from it. Of course, in the case of foliage decoration, this is exactly what it does! Let the form of the letter influence your drawing by echoing the shapes of the letter. Restraint is important—less is often better.

LEFT: *Decoration can be used around letters. In all cases, the basic form of the letter should be retained and not destroyed by illumination.*

RIGHT: *Decoration can be applied to the actual lines of the letter.*

GILDING

Unless the actual letter or letters are to be gilded, it is best to leave the application of gold to the end and apply it sparingly to the design. The simplest way to do this is to use the gold paint supplied in the kit. However, if you would like to try raised gilding, the following method is the simplest. You will have to purchase real gold leaf from an art materials supplier. You will also need PVA adhesive—the sort that is flexible when dry. A burnisher (made from agate or stainless steel) is also necessary, although the rounded side of a smooth teaspoon can be used instead.

Using a fine brush, paint the shape with PVA, thinned with water if necessary. It makes it easier to see the PVA against white paper if you add a very small amount of artists' watercolor to it. Avoid bubbles and aim for a smooth, even, rounded finish. When this is completely dry, breathe on it for a few seconds—this should make it tacky. Carefully apply the gold leaf with the protective tissue on top and press very firmly. Using a burnisher, rub over the tissue. The gold should stick to the PVA. Remove the tissue and carefully burnish directly on the gold. You can repeat the process several times to patch missing areas, but it becomes more difficult to get the gold to stick with each attempt.

1 *Carefully draw the outline of the letter or shape that is to be gilded.*

2 *Apply the PVA ground to the letter, making sure that there are no bubbles and that the finished surface is smooth.*

3 *When the PVA is dry, lay the gold leaf over the letter and press down firmly.*

4 *Polish the gold with a burnisher or the rounded side of a teaspoon.*

page layout
and decoration

 our design may comprise a single illuminated letter or a page with one or more illuminated letters and some text. A single letter can be located centrally on the page—or anywhere else for that matter. When you have several elements—illuminated letters and text blocks, as well as other decoration—your layout has to be given greater consideration.

There is one simple principle of page layout—everything should look as if it is where it is meant to be. In other words, layout should look "designed." However, the best layouts will not be noticed. There are several ways to achieve an effective design. The most difficult is to arrange the elements until they appear to be "right." To get the correct balance of scale, proportion, weight, color, and so on, takes skill and experience. A much simpler way is to construct a grid and fit the elements within the grid so that there is some sort of linear relationship between them.

Think of decoration as illustration, not in the sense that it portrays some figurative image, but as something that complements the lettering and the subject of the text in both style and content. The elements of illumination range from realistic paintings of figures, animals, and plants to the most

u'il soit calligraphié ou typographié, un texte possède sa propre texture visuelle. il est frappant de vour à quel point l'aspect global d'un texte peut être affecté par d'infimes changements, que ce soit dans la densité, la hauteur ou la largeur de la lettre, dans le jeu des pleins et des déliés, dans la forme des obits et des empattements, ou encore dans l'esplacement des lettres et des lignes.

ABOVE: *Separate elements in a design can be arranged more easily if they fit within a grid. This is a very simple example in which the "Q" and the decoration make use of a grid to determine their position on the page.*

abstract geometric patterns. Somewhere in between lies heraldry, which often combines more or less realistic designs with simple shapes and abstract patterns, frequently incorporating gold and silver.

Decoration, such as borders, can be used to combine or hold together the elements of a layout, but try to design the layout so that it works without the addition of a border and use it as an enhancement afterward. Simple borders are often the best. Even a single fine line around a layout can be more effective than the most elaborate floral border. Another way to help hold layouts together is to use color washes behind the lettering. Illumination does not have to be "hard-edged" and traditional— be creative and develop your own ideas from the principles presented here.

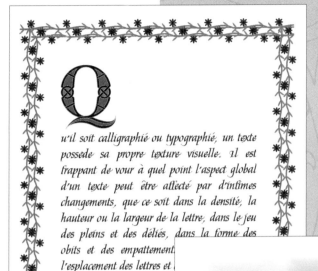

u'il soit calligraphié ou typographié, un texte possede sa propre texture visuelle. il est frappant de vour à quel point l'aspect global d'un texte peut être affecté par d'infimes changements, que ce soit dans la densité, la hauteur ou la largeur de la lettre, dans le jeu des pleins et des déliés, dans la forme des obits et des empattement, l'esplacement des lettres et

LEFT: *Decorative borders can be used to enhance a design, but try to design a good layout considering the addition of a border.*

BELOW: *A simple watercolor wash behind lettering can sometimes be effective.*

u'il soit calligraphié ou typographié, un texte possede sa propre texture visuelle. il est frappant de vour à quel point l'aspect global d'un texte peut être affecté par d'infimes changements, que ce soit dans la densité, la hauteur ou la largeur de la lettre, dans le jeu des pleins et des déliés, dans la forme des obits et des empattements, ou encore dans l'esplacement des lettres et des lignes.

PART THREE

exercises and projects

THE FOLLOWING PROJECTS WILL GIVE
YOU SOME PRACTICE AND DEVELOP
YOUR SKILLS. EACH IS PROGRESSIVELY
MORE COMPLEX, BUT EVEN THE FINAL
PROJECT IS ACHIEVABLE BY ANYONE.
WORK THROUGH EACH PROJECT IN
TURN SO THAT YOU GRASP THE
TECHNIQUES AS THEY BECOME MORE
DIFFICULT. IF YOU FIND THAT YOU ARE
LEARNING QUICKLY, YOU MAY WISH TO
ADAPT OR ENHANCE THE PROJECTS TO
SUIT YOUR OWN TASTES.

SHORT INTRODUCTORY PROJECT

You should be able to complete every one of the projects using the materials supplied in the kit. However, several more advanced processes and materials are suggested in some of them, especially the final project. These should direct you to the next steps in illuminated lettering. The additional materials can be purchased or ordered from good artists' materials stores. In every case, an alternative using the supplied media is given.

This short introductory project takes you through some simple basic steps involved in drawing and painting lines and shapes. It also demonstrates a good way to make tracings, which you may find very useful in the projects.

Although not strictly illuminated lettering, heraldry is very much an aspect of illumination. Drawing and painting a heraldic device (or coat of arms) is a very good discipline that involves both straight lines and geometric shapes. Follow the steps as they are described.

LEFT: *Illuminated heraldry appears in many different locations and not always on paper or vellum. Here, bright gold and rich colors are used on a stone-carved coat of arms in Brugge, Belgium.*

1 *Using a medium soft pencil, lightly draw a shield shape. This doesn't have to be exactly as illustrated, but make the proportions similar. If you have a long rule and compass, you can use these to draw the lines and curves. Divide the shield into four quarters as shown. When you are happy with the pencil drawing, carefully draw over it with the tip of your brush or, if you have one, a long rule for the straight lines.*

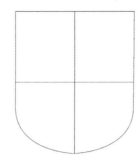

A simple way to make a tracing is to use thin, translucent (layout) paper together with a soft and hard pencil. Lay the paper over the image to be traced. Trace the outline of the image using the soft pencil. Don't press too hard, or you could damage the original. Turn the paper over and cover the underside using the soft pencil.

2 *Trace or copy four versal letters from the alphabet illustrated on page 35. They don't have to be "ABVY"—decide on your own.*

Lay the paper face up in the position where you want the image to be. It is a good idea to tape it down with painter's tape. Draw over the original traced shape using the hard pencil, pressing fairly firmly. This will transfer the image to the paper below. Any unwanted marks can be removed with a soft eraser.

3 *Carefully color the first letter in the top left of the shield. Use a simple pure, flat color. Use all the hairs of the brush for the thick lines and the point for the fine lines. Note that the more carefully you have drawn the letter, the easier it will be to color it.*

4 *Now color the letter in the lower right quarter of the shield, using a different pure, flat color.*

ABOVE: *Using all the hairs of the brush helps to keep a smooth edge to the line.*

ABOVE: *Fine lines can be painted with the point of the brush.*

5 *Color the remaining two letters, either with your gold paint or with yellow (to represent gold).*

6 *When you are sure that the paint is dry, color the background of the first two letters that you filled, using black ink.*

We will now add a very simple linear design below the shield. Designs of this sort are very common in both heraldry and illuminated lettering, so practice in creating these shapes will pay off.

7 *Draw an outline similar to that shown in the illustration. Your design doesn't have to be identical, nor does the left and right side need to be same. However, they must be visually balanced. You can make the thorny projections longer than in the illustration if you want a richer effect. You can even add leaves or flowers. Try to maintain flowing lines throughout.*

10 *The design is complete, but you may wish to try an improved version with the shield overlapping the linear patterns and with the addition of a second outline to the shield. You could also try adding some decoration of your own above the shield.*

8 *Copy your design (using the tracing technique previously described) and draw a "flipped" version over the first. Add some small circles to the end points to enhance the decoration.*

9 *Color the linear design with gold paint or yellow. Paint the little circles red.*

PROJECT ONE

a Bookmark

(BY MAUREEN SULLIVAN)

*A bookmark can be designed in a
number of ways. It could include
anything from a simple border pattern
to a more complex design.
A person's name could be written down
the length of the bookmark, or, as in this
project, a large decorated letter could be
used. The letter is based on a versal form
and then adapted for the bookmark. You
have already learned that there are many
examples of illuminated letters from
which you can seek inspiration. For this
project, the bowl of the "P" has been
made rather narrow, as a normally
proportioned letter could look odd in a
long, thinnish bookmark.*

RIGHT: *The bookmark,
complete with tassel.*

1 *Begin by sketching out some ideas with a pencil. Think about the size and shape you would like your bookmark to be. Explore the possibilities of how large you would like the decorated letter. For example, you might decide to have a small letter at the top of the bookmark and a border pattern around the sides.*

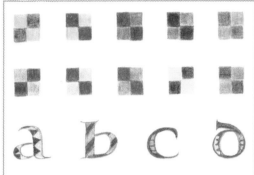

ABOVE: *Try out different color schemes using color pencils or paint.*

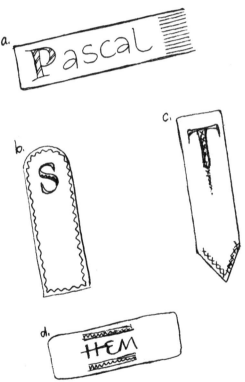

RIGHT: *Make small thumbnail sketches to develop ideas for the shape and design of the bookmark.*

2 *You can either follow the colors given in the project or choose your own. You could try experimenting with color pencils to find different color combinations. It is advisable to limit the palette to two or three colors at this stage.*

3 Once you are satisfied with your design, or if you are going to follow the project, trace it and carefully transfer it onto the supplied cartridge paper. If you want a thicker and stronger bookmark, use a heavyweight hot pressed watercolor paper (available from artists' stores). If the tracing is a little faint, go over the lines with a pencil.

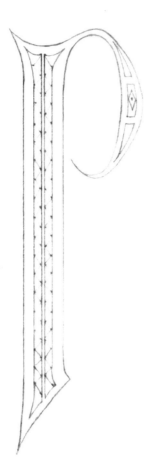

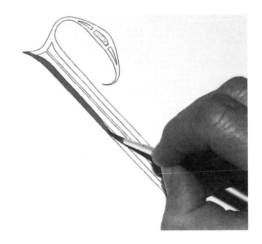

4 The colors used in the project are blue, green, and gold. Mix each color in a separate palette (a small saucer will do) with a clean brush. Add a few drops of water at a time and mix to a thin creamy consistency. Green can be mixed by using equal quantities of the blue and yellow colors that are supplied with the kit. For painting, you can use the brush supplied in the way that has already been described, or you can use two brushes—a larger one for the larger areas of color and a very small one for the fine lines and detail.

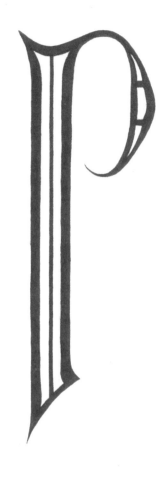

6 *Dip your brush into the blue paint, then wipe the excess off the brush against the side of the palette. Now you can begin to fill in the large areas of blue. Start at the top of the letter near an outside line but not actually on it. You can then gradually tease the brush nearer and nearer the line. If you find it patchy when it has dried, you might like to give it a second coat. It is a good idea to cover all of the work, except the small area you are painting, with a piece of protective paper.*

5 *Before you actually begin the project, you might find it helpful to practice painting a few thin lines. Draw a few sets of parallel lines ⅛ inch (3mm) apart and a few more at less than ¹⁄₁₆ inch (1mm) apart. Using the point of the brush, slowly and carefully pull it downward for a half-inch or so, then put the brush back into the wet paint and draw downward again. Repeat this down the other side and then fill in the middle. Don't worry if you wobble over the lines at first; it will get better with practice. The inner lines can be retouched later, but you won't want to retouch with white paint on the outside margin of the letter, so be more careful with that part.*

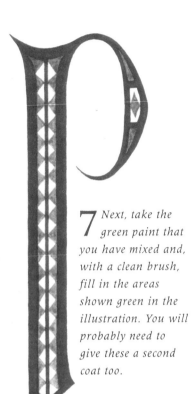

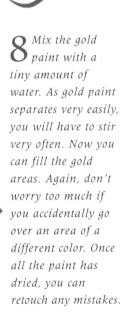

7 *Next, take the green paint that you have mixed and, with a clean brush, fill in the areas shown green in the illustration. You will probably need to give these a second coat too.*

8 *Mix the gold paint with a tiny amount of water. As gold paint separates very easily, you will have to stir very often. Now you can fill the gold areas. Again, don't worry too much if you accidentally go over an area of a different color. Once all the paint has dried, you can retouch any mistakes.*

9 *Just the last little details to paint now. Dip your brush into the blue paint and wipe as much excess paint off as possible. On a spare piece of paper, try painting some very thin lines. Now add the blue lines to the green and gold triangles. Paint the blue dots on the green, and add the gold lines around the shapes on the bowl of the "P."*

10 *With a long rule and a snap-blade knife, carefully cut out the bookmark. The illustration shows the completed bookmark with a tassel attached. You could hang any other kind of memento on it if you wish. If you are going to do this, punch a hole through which it can be threaded. At this stage, you might decide to get your bookmark laminated, or spray it with a fixative in case any color rubs off onto the page of the book. Once this has been done, you can thread the tassel or memento through the hole and you now have a handmade, decorated bookmark of which you can be proud.*

RIGHT: *The bookmark, complete with tassel.*

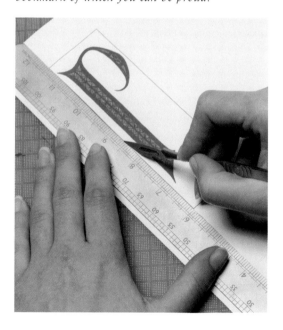

PROJECT TWO

a gift box and tag

(BY MAUREEN SULLIVAN)

The richness of gold embellishment imparts a splendor to the page. Most calligraphers have admired the fine gilding in medieval manuscripts and wish to try their own hand at some form of gilding. Some techniques are easy and some are more technically demanding. Find a method suitable for you.

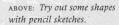

ABOVE: *Try out some shapes with pencil sketches.*

1 t is not only in manuscript books that illumination can be applied. There are many ways in which gifts and other objects can be decorated and illuminated. The application can range from simple ideas to much more complex designs. This project explores some ideas for decorating a gift box with a matching gift tag. A presentation gift box and gift tag, which has been designed for special occasion, adds a sentimental value to the gift. The recipient is sure to express delight at such a thoughtful and personal present. There are craft boxes available in a variety of shapes and sizes, which can be purchased to suit your gift. These can be painted and decorated using your own color schemes and designs.

1 *Begin by making some thumbnail sketches of suitable designs for the top of the gift box and gift tag. The tag will probably be much smaller than the box, so you could select an element of the overall design for it. For example, use the person's initials on the tag and the whole name on the box. When sketching your ideas, try to reflect in the design the purpose for which the gift box is intended.*

2 *If you are thinking of introducing some writing and color with gold adornment, it is a good idea to make some color trials at this stage, as it may affect the final presentation of the box. Try writing out the words you have chosen in different styles and sizes. Use different nib sizes, if you have more than one. For a baby's christening gift, for example, you may choose to use an italic form of writing with a fairly narrow nib. This would give the design an appropriately delicate look, whereas the use of something like a gothic hand would make the appearance too strong and heavy in this context.*

Experiment with a variety of colors for your design. The color of your pen-written words will look different from the solid color mixed in your palette. Compare your writing with a variety of small and large nibs and notice how the color changes. Write your trials on the type of paper you intend using for the project. The color and texture of paper varies a great deal, and this can surprisingly alter the color of your paint. These trials can be done quickly and roughly, but it will give you a clearer idea of how your finished artwork will look.

Assembling the design

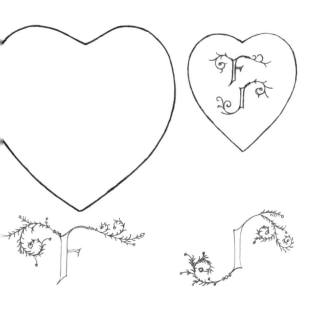

4 *Transfer the tracings onto paper. Use the paper supplied with the kit or choose another if you wish. It will be much easier to write and decorate on the paper than on the box lid. Write out the words you have chosen in a good strong color, leaving the initial letter or letters clear that are to be gilded. Remember to keep the rest of your work covered to avoid accidental marks.*

LEFT: *Carefully trace the design elements that you have selected.*

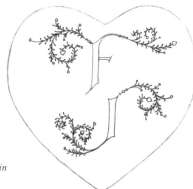

RIGHT: *Transfer the tracings onto paper in their final position.*

3 *When you are happy with the designs of both the box and tag, transfer them onto tracing paper. Take the lid of the box you have chosen, then turn it upside down onto the paper or card and trace around the lid. Place the tracing over this shape and move it around until you are happy with the position. Depending on the size of the box or tag, it may be necessary to reduce or enlarge your design to fit, ideally with a photocopier, if you have access to one.*

RIGHT: *Write the lettering using a suitable color.*

5 Now paint the large initial letters with gold paint (or if you wish, try some gilding with gold leaf). Outline the shape of the letter carefully with the paint and then flood in the center of the letter. The paint should then dry evenly and smoothly.

6 The decoration can now be added using the pointed pen or the point of the brush. Use the gold paint mixed to a thin, creamy consistency, and stir it often. Use the tip of the brush and make short overlapping strokes to paint the lines.

7 Using the same color as used for the writing, add the two little hearts to the large initial letters. Then add the red decorative details.

8 When all the paint has dried, carefully cut around the heart shape (or the shape you have chosen). Next, paint a thin border around the edge of the heart with gold paint. Place the heart shape centrally on the lid, then check the position and lightly mark with a pencil. Paste the area within the pencil mark and lay the heart-shaped artwork onto the lid, then cover with some tissue and press the edges down until stuck.

RIGHT: *Apply the gold paint to the areas that are to be gilded. If you are using gold leaf, apply the ground and lay down the gold at this point.*

Completing the boxes

9 *The gift box is now ready for any further decoration you may wish to add, such as a ribbon around the box and (if the box is sufficiently large) a bow or flower on the lid.*

10 *Finally, the gift tag can be made in the same way, but on a smaller scale, using the design of the gift box, which has been simplified. For example, modify the design by using only the two initials. The gift tag shape can be cut out and a tiny hole punched to place some ribbon or cord through. Alternatively, if you wish the gift tag to be a folded card, trace two heart shapes side by side and cut them out, leaving ½ inch (5 mm) uncut to make the join. Carefully fold the card in two and then, if you like, add a ribbon or cord.*

All that is left to do now is to place the gift in your beautiful presentation box and write a personal message on the gift tag.

LEFT: *The completed gift box and tag. The beautiful lettering is very eye-catching.*

RIGHT: *Some alternative completed gift box and tag designs.*

PROJECT THREE

a greeting card

(BY MAUREEN SULLIVAN)

In project one, bright, bold colors were used to embellish an initial letter, while in project two the emphasis was on the use of gold paint (or flat gilding) with just a small amount of color added to the decoration. All these elements will now be combined to create a rich and colorful illuminated design. You'll need the gold paint for this project. A touch of gold can bring a page to life!

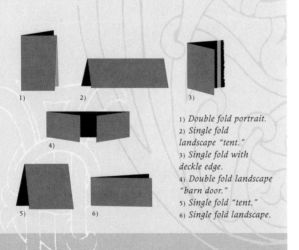

1) *Double fold portrait.*
2) *Single fold landscape "tent."*
3) *Single fold with deckle edge.*
4) *Double fold landscape "barn door."*
5) *Single fold "tent."*
6) *Single fold landscape.*

*T*here is something very special about sending a handmade greeting card. Before you begin the project, here are some simple exercises and trials to help you experiment with your ideas and give you some advice and tips on techniques used in producing a card.

EXERCISES

Card folds

There are many shapes and sizes you can choose for your card. Do remember to fit the card to an envelope. There is nothing worse than spending many hours on your greeting card just to find that you cannot obtain an envelope to put it in. Make some thumbnail sketches of your ideas and think about the size and shape of card you would like to make. Take a sheet of letter size paper. This is the standard size used for typing. Fold this sheet in half, and you will have a large single fold card. If you need a large area for your design, this could be an ideal size. Fold the sheet in half again, and you will have a double-fold card.

The options for sizes and shapes of cards are endless. A few suggestions to experiment with are shown on the left.

Borders and patterns using a pen

There is a variety of ways in which a simple pattern or border can be used to great effect with illumination. In historical manuscripts, you will often see a decorative border "trailing" from a versal or initial letter. This can take a naturalistic form such as flowers and leaves, a delicate filigree drawn with a thin pen nib, or painted patterned borders ranging from simple to extremely elaborate designs.

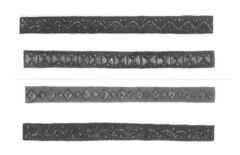

ABOVE: *Practice "drawing" these borders with your broad-edged pen and the point of your brush.*

A border can be used quite separately from the illuminated letter. For example, it can be used to make a vertical edge to the side of the card or as a box or corners to "frame" the card. Try some penmade patterns of your own. Use your broad-edge calligraphy pen to draw some patterns quite freely. Ideas will soon flow. Then try painting some borders. Some will work better than others. Choose whichever you think would suit your overall design. Copy the examples in the illustration and create some of your own.

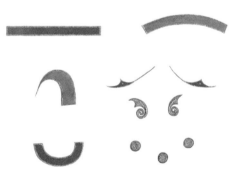

BELOW: *The characteristics of a shape change when they are outlined in color or gold.*

Outlining a design

Perhaps you will have noticed that illuminations and miniatures are often outlined in order to define the detail. This is usually the last stage when completing a piece of work and it can be a little daunting to keep a steady hand while outlining with a thin brush. Therefore, it is worth spending a few minutes practicing before commencing the final stage. You will soon feel more relaxed and gain confidence. Use gold paint and the tip of your brush. Wipe the excess paint from the brush and try outlining some circles and shapes as shown in the examples.

ABOVE: *Try to keep the PVA within the pencil lines.*

ABOVE: *A second layer may be added.*

ABOVE: *"Pull" the PVA with the tip of the brush into the corners.*

ABOVE: *If the gold has not adhered to the ground, add another coat and apply more gold when it is dry.*

ABOVE: *Two or more layers will give a raised effect.*

ABOVE: *Make sure that you apply pressure with your burnisher right to the edges of the shape.*

ABOVE: *Well-laid and burnished gold should be very smooth and bright.*

Gold leaf practice

If you plan to use gold leaf in this, or any of the other projects, it is worth spending a little time practicing applying the PVA ground and laying the gold. These short exercises will help you get a feel for the medium. PVA behaves differently from watercolor paints, unless it is made much thinner by adding water. The thicker the PVA used for a ground for gilding, the brighter and more effective the gold will be.

1 Draw small circles, dots, and squares with a pencil. Fill the shapes with PVA and try applying a second coat to build up the thickness of the ground. Practice "drawing out" the PVA to a fine point.

2 Practice applying the gold leaf. The first application may not cover the ground completely and a second layer can be applied. However, the more you try to apply additional layers of gold, the more difficult it will be to get it to stick to the ground.

3 Practice burnishing the gold. The thin gold leaf is surprisingly strong and you can build up considerable pressure on your burnisher, spoon, or silk. However, the ground must be perfectly smooth or you will tear the gold surface. Any bubbles in the PVA will create a real problem at this stage.

THE PROJECT

For the greeting card in this project, the monogram "MA" is taken from *The Lindisfarne Gospels*. However, in this project the monogram is used and embellished in a more contemporary style. Begin by making some rough sketches of your design ideas and decide on the size and shape of your card and envelope. Experiment with colors to suit your greeting card or follow the set project. If you have followed projects one and two, you should be able to develop your own ideas without further guidance.

1 *Once you have decided upon all the details, draw up and transfer your design onto tracing paper. Now transfer your design onto the paper or card you have chosen to use, taking account of the fold or folds. Leave plenty of extra card or paper around your design to allow for trimming.*

2 *Apply the gold paint to those areas shown on the MA monogram and in the box. Alternatively, apply the transfer gold leaf to flat and raised PVA bases. Keep all your work covered, apart from the area you are gilding. If you are using gold leaf, pay particular attention to the edges to make sure the gold has stuck, and leave for a few hours before burnishing.*

ABOVE: *Work out all the elements of the design, then trace it as you've done in the previous projects.*

RIGHT: *Make sure that the gold goes right to the edge of the shapes.*

3 *Mix your blue and red paint to make purple and add a little white. Paint the large letter "M." Now mix your blue and yellow paint to make green and then paint the large "A" using green, a little yellow, and a touch of white. Outline the letter and, with a loaded brush, quickly fill in the shape. This should help the paint to dry flat and even.*

4 *Take a little of the purple mix (keeping the rest) and add more white to make a lighter purple or mauve, then carefully paint the border surrounding the name.*

5 *Fill in the letters between the gold. Paint alternate letters with the green and purple mixes. Make sure the painted letter is dry before covering it and moving on to the next.*

6 *Now with gold paint, outline the "M" and "A." Apply short overlapping strokes with a fine brush. Keep your eye closely on the outside of the letter as a guide. The inside edge can be retouched later with green or purple if you wobble too much. Add the tiny gold dots for decoration.*

7 Carefully mark up the final size of the card in pencil and trim it with a snap-blade knife. Score that card where it is to be folded using the blunt side of a knife blade or similar object. This will create a much sharper fold. You can embellish the card with the addition of a ribbon or other decoration. All that remains now is for you to write a personal message inside your beautifully illuminated greeting card.

BELOW: *The completed design with the addition of a ribbon.*

LEFT: *A very delicate letterform drawn with a very narrow nib and gilded in the counters of the letters.*

BELOW: *A single letter and borders in this design create an effective contrast with the deckle edge of the paper.*

Other suggestions

In this project, we have given instructions based on the name "Maureen" and the monogram "MA." The design was a modern interpretation of eighth-century letterforms. You can experiment with many other approaches and design styles, which need not derive from early manuscripts. The examples illustrated here demonstrate the variety of illuminated letterforms that can be created, including some which are of a much less formal style.

BELOW: *A very informal and almost humorous approach to lettering and illumination has been taken in this card.*

ABOVE: *In this design, gold paint has been used to outline the letter "T" and in the border.*

illuminated lettering for framing

(BY JANET MEHIGAN)

The illuminated Latin motto that forms this project is the most complex piece of work in the book. Read the exercises and practice carefully to ensure that you get an attractive, confident result. Use the gold paint supplied in the pack to highlight your design or, if you're feeling especially confident, you can experiment with real gold.

Y ou can use the colors supplied with the kit, so where a specific color is mentioned either use the paints provided in your kit or, if you want to treat the design in a more advanced way, purchase Winsor Blue, Winsor Green, white, spectrum yellow, cadmium red, and cobalt blue.

EXERCISES

Decorating a letter

Successful design of a project is about using various elements of a composition and arranging them in a pleasing and expressive way to convey meaning either with the words or pictorially, or both. Often an idea will come to mind and you then have the difficult task of interpreting it onto paper. Having looked at historical manuscripts and admired the decorative and illuminated letters and bright miniature paintings, you will want to use these ideas. The possibilities are endless.

We have seen that the versal letter was used as an initial decorative letter. Practice writing these multistroke letters with your pen. In the historical manuscripts, they were often drawn larger and colored in red, but sometimes green and blue. You can do the same by using your colored paint. These letters can be used as the first letter to begin a verse in poetry and, to add simple interest, can be made larger and colored and decorated with paint. Any artistic work can be enhanced by color and writing, illustration or symbolism, and illumination.

Draw the letter "C" with a pen and ink, copying it from the versal exemplar on page 35. Prepare some paint in red, blue, and green.

1 Draw a versal "C" using red paint in your pen, filling the stem center with the same color, or fill the center of the letter stem with a contrasting color.

2 To add interest, fill in the center of the letter (counter space) with blue.

3 Try some other letters such as "D," "H," and "M," using blue and green.

4 To make the letter design more effective, create a checker design within the center, and paint alternating checkers in blue and red gouache. The white filigree design is added with the careful use of white paint and a tip of your brush.

Simple decorative additions

Now let us take the lettering designs a bit further.

You can further develop your ideas by looking at the Celtic designs and using them to decorate the inside counter space of your letters and using several colors.

5 *Using your pen, draw the versal letter "A." On the right-hand side, the stem has two bars. This is achieved by drawing each downward stroke twice (or use a larger nib).*

6 *Add serif extensions and change the cross bar.*

7 *Try changing the letter by exaggerating the shape and adding further filigree extensions and contrasting color to the left-hand side of the letter.*

8 *The uncial letter "D" adapted from letters in* The Lindisfarne Gospels.

9 *The uncial letter "B," based on letters used in* The Lindisfarne Gospels. *The dots are added with a pen using red paint.*

Adding more design

The patterns used for decoration can become as complicated or innovative as you wish. Letters can be placed in square boxes and oval shapes. You will find many ideas by looking at historical manuscripts, but you can easily invent your own.

ABOVE: *Letter "U" painted with an outline of gold. A mixture of blue and white has been used to paint the center stem of the letter, with white for the highlighted decoration.*

RIGHT: *Letter "A" with decoration in the stem. The letter has been drawn in outline in red paint with a triangular pattern added. Gold and red paint have been used to decorate. White paint has been used on the first "A" to add further interest.*

FAR LEFT: *Letter "O" painted in gold.*

LEFT MIDDLE: *Gold letter "O" placed inside a cobalt blue (or a mix of blue and white) painted square with white decoration.*

LEFT: *Using white paint, further filigree decoration is added.*

Adding a border

Decoration need not be confined to the letter only but can be incorporated into a border design. In this way, a whole page can be designed with calligraphy, a large decorated letter, and a border design to enhance the whole piece of work. It will need some initial planning, but will be very satisfying when completed. The border design can be just decoration or reflect what the text is about. Here are some ideas for you to try, and then you can invent some of your own.

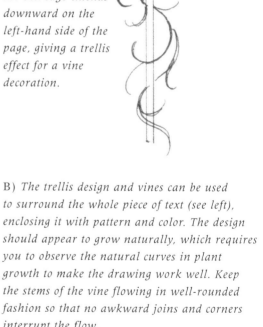

A) *This is a design for the letter "T," which contains a simple stem pattern and has been placed within a box. By using different colors and gold paint, many variations on this idea can be made. In addition, the box edge extends downward on the left-hand side of the page, giving a trellis effect for a vine decoration.*

B) *The trellis design and vines can be used to surround the whole piece of text (see left), enclosing it with pattern and color. The design should appear to grow naturally, which requires you to observe the natural curves in plant growth to make the drawing work well. Keep the stems of the vine flowing in well-rounded fashion so that no awkward joins and corners interrupt the flow.*

C) *This stylized leaf design can be painted in gold, and the bar on which it is climbing can be in gold or color.*

D) *A geometric design where colors or gold can be alternated.*

E) *A Celtic knot design. This is intricate, but makes a good border design.*

F) *A simple leaf design.*

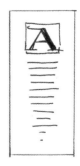

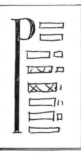

ABOVE: *These are some small thumbnail sketches of project ideas using a capital letter and text.*

Organizing your layout

The design possibilities of using text with an illuminated letter are endless and you will need to sketch a number of ideas in pencil to enable you to plan. These small drawings do not have to be detailed at this stage, so do not be inhibited by careful writing or exact measurements. Just scribble down the ideas you may have in your head. Once on paper, it is amazing how these little drawings help to stimulate other ideas. The finished design may be made from one of these thumbnail sketches only, but could just as easily develop from a combination of ideas and elements from the other sketches.

A) *This Latin quotation can be given as a framed piece of work. It could have a gilded letter "O" containing a heart and be surrounded by a very decorative border containing gold flowers and leaves.*

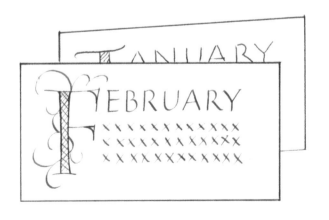

B) *This shows what could be pages from a calendar book, featuring a decorated and illuminated capital for each of the months of the year. The pages of the book could be held together with ribbons through punched holes.*

C) *This design could be placed on a card. The capital "L" would be gold on a blue background.*

D) *This simple design "Usus est magister optimus," means "Practice makes perfect," and it has been chosen for the main part of the project, with some extra decoration and gold.*

THE PROJECT

On your paper, plan where the illuminated letter and writing are going to be. Rule up the paper with your writing guidelines, leaving a space for your decorative letter and border designs.

When executing a design that contains color, gold, and writing, it is wise to do your writing first. The writing is where most of the mistakes are made. It is much easier to write it a second time should this occur than to do the gilding and painting again.

The gold paint supplied with the kit can be used throughout this next project, but you may wish to try applying real gold, or even use a mixture of both.

For the writing in this project, you can use a script of your choice or, as here, gothic script. You can refer to the gothic script on pages 36 to 37 as a guide for the project.

1 Carefully write out the text below. Practice measuring the nib width(s) for your writing and drawing the correct guidelines for your work. When you are satisfied that it is what you want, write it on your paper. When it is dry, cover it with a paper guard for protection.

BELOW: *Draw your guidelines lightly and accurately in pencil, then write the lettering.*

magister

optimus.

Practice makes perfect

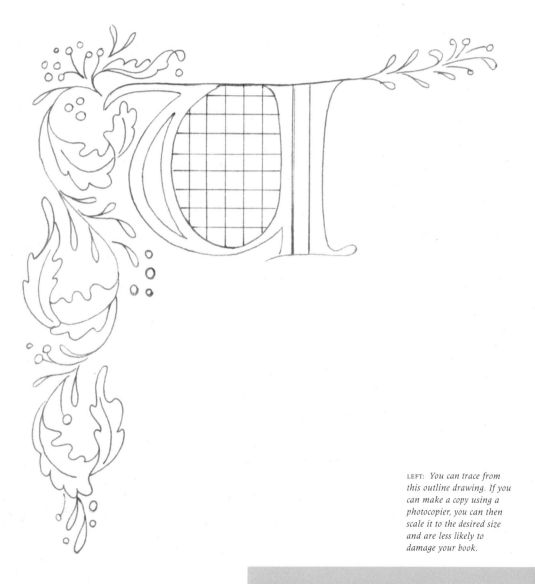

ABOVE: *By using tracings, you can easily adjust the positions of the elements in the design until they are perfectly placed.*

Adding gold and color

In the descriptions that follow, colors are specified. You can modify the designs and use your own color scheme if you have only a limited range available. Remember that blue and yellow make green, red and yellow make orange, and blue and red make purple.

2 *Trace the letter and border design. Transfer it to your piece of paper in the appropriate position and trace down. Decide whether you are going to use the gold paint supplied, or real gold. Note how well the mixture of lettering styles works. The contrast between the uncial "U" and the gothic and italic script is effective and quite dramatic. When you use different lettering together, make sure that they are very different in style, size, or color as in this piece. If styles and sizes are too close, they will look like mistakes.*

ABOVE: *You can create almost any color by mixing the primary red, yellow, and blue. However, pure primary colors and simple mixes as shown here are by far the most effective in illumination.*

4 *You are now ready to paint. Carefully mask with protective paper areas not to be painted. Using blue with a touch of white, mix a midblue color to paint the checker design in the center of the illuminated letter. Always mix plenty of gouache colors, as it is impossible to mix the exact same color twice. Any color remaining can be kept covered and then reconstituted with water for use later. Paint a diamond pattern on the blue squares in the center of the letter, using white with a small touch of blue added to tone it down fractionally.*

3 *Paint the letter with the gold paint or apply the ground for gilding and lay down the gold as described earlier in the book.*

LEFT: *Gold paint will not give you the brilliance of real gold leaf, but it is much easier to apply and is much less expensive.*

RIGHT: *The design is now beginning to take shape.*

Completing the design

5 *Paint in the border design using a green and yellow mix. This will create a flat midgreen color. Let dry. Now you can begin to make darker and lighter tones in the painting. Mix more blue with some of the midgreen to add the shadows on the design. Add white to the midgreen to create highlights. Build up the shadows and highlights separately by using small strokes with the tip of your brush. This will make the design three-dimensional.*

6 *Add further colors to your design in the same way. Now that you have finished your project, you can place a mount (or two mounts of contrasting color) around it and frame it.*

LEFT: *Carefully copy the coloring and shading as shown here to create a three-dimensional effect in the foliated design.*

RIGHT: *The completed illuminated lettering.*

Usus est magister optimus.

Practice makes perfect

templates and tracing designs

The following pages should help you to prepare your very own illuminated document. Here you will find some introductory ideas for layout, decorative initial letters, borders, and patterns, which you can incorporate in your designs. You should soon begin to develop your own original ways of doing things. One of the best ways to learn is from examples. You will find many more in other books and, of course, in original illuminated manuscripts.

LEFT: *A single justified column of text with the illuminated letter above.*

RIGHT: *The same document shown in an unjustified arrangement with the enlarged letter set into the beginning of the text.*

LAYOUT TEMPLATES

We have already emphasized the importance of planning your layouts properly so that everything looks "right." The illustrations show some of the principal ways of arranging text together with an illuminated initial letter or letters. Text can either be justified, with the right margin straight, or unjustified with the right margin "ragged," sometimes called "ragged right." The choice is yours: Justified text looks more formal. Poetry will always have an uneven right margin. The initial illuminated letter can be kept separate from the text block, either in the left margin or above, or it can be set into the text, either partially or completely.

If you have enough text, it can be arranged in two or more columns with the same alternative ways of using initial letters. However, if you would like to be much more creative, the illuminated initial letter could be placed centrally in the document with the text surrounding it. Alternatively, a single text column could be split above and below a greatly enlarged letter.

RIGHT: *A two-column design with several enlarged initial letters.*

LEFT: *A two-column layout with the initial letters set into the margins.*

RIGHT: *An enlarged centralized initial letter with surrounding text.*

LEFT: *A single text column split above and below the enlarged letter.*

sample
initial letters

You may already be keen to develop your own ideas and to try a more advanced illuminated letter. It is perfectly permissible to develop your ideas from examples that you admire and to adapt them to your own requirements. There are two main sources of inspiration—historical manuscripts and contemporary typefaces.

The early examples illustrated are from an eighteenth-century book, *The Origin and Progress of Writing* by Thomas Astle, and are his interpretations of medieval letters. You probably will not want to make your letters so elaborate, but you can borrow many of their elements and utilize them in your own way.

RIGHT: *The letter "V" formed of two fictitious creatures from* Caedmon's Poetical Paraphrase *of the books of Genesis and Daniel (from Astle).*

BELOW: *A humanist italic typeface with script-like capitals (Vivaldi).*

For example, you could use the spiral shapes, the interlace design, or the terminal animal heads in the "DI" design that has been modified from a sixth-century manuscript. You may wish to take ideas from the ninth-century "D" or even make up letters entirely from plants or animals as in the tenth century "V."

Decorative typefaces are ideal sources for the basic forms of illuminated letters. Even more modern "sans serif" designs can be good starting points. Some of the "display" typefaces will provide you with ideas for you to enhance the letters by the addition of elaborate flourishes, just as in the gothic example given here. Remember to retain the basic forms of the letters when you develop your illumination ideas.

LEFT: *A simple, elegant contemporary typeface, useful for a modern application (Eras Light).*

LEFT: *A gothic-style display typeface with elaborate flourishes (Parchment).*

85 *Sample initial letters*

BORDERS AND PATTERNS

BELOW: *The simplest of borders based on a zigzag, filled to create triangles.*

BELOW: *A double zigzag pattern creating diamond shapes in reverse (negative).*

BELOW: *A wavy line repeat—more difficult to draw.*

BELOW: *An oval repeat border based on a repeat of a double wavy line.*

Designs that are composed of repeated elements have a strong visual impact. Both borders and textural patterns that can be incorporated into illuminated lettering are often formed from a repeated pattern. Sometimes this is geometric, but sometimes the repeated element is a complex, perhaps figurative or floral shape.

Borders can be used to enhance or decorate a part of a layout or the whole design. Take care that the border does not become more dominant than the content—let your illumination shine through. Even the simplest of shapes, such as squares and triangles, take on a whole new effect when repeated as a regular border. Experiment with positive and negative effects and with color. Repeated curved linear, circular, or oval shapes can be a little more difficult to draw, but may be more appropriate in some situations.

Geometric fill patterns can be used with your illuminated lettering. They are commonly found in heraldry, but can also be used to add textural effect to the letters or their counters. Patterns of this sort will usually give a contemporary look to illumination, although similar designs can be found in the earliest illuminated manuscripts. As with borders, changing from positive to negative can change the whole appearance of the design.

Practice drawing simple geometric repeat patterns, as this will help you when designing illuminated borders and textural areas based on much more complex elements such as flowers and leaves.

ABOVE: *Example of border or pattern in an illuminated letter from fourteenth century* (Pilgrims of Santiago de Compostela), *on vellum.*

RIGHT: *Sample repeat patterns. These can be modified in various ways, such as positive to negative or by using color, to create quite different effects.*

foliated designs

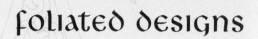

1 llumination often utilizes textures or decoration based on plants. These are termed "foliated" patterns or designs. A grasp of the principles of geometric repeats is fundamental to designing these patterns, but equally important is an understanding of how plants grow, how they branch, where the leaves form, and the shapes and structures of the leaves themselves.

Study books on plants and flowers. Note how stems branch from the main shoot, then other slightly thinner shoot branches from it, and so

LEFT: *Opposite leaf growth form and alternate leaf growth form.*

RIGHT: *A foliated design. Note how the design is carefully balanced and is based on a very simple growth form.*

RIGHT: *Woodcuts from Gerard's Herbal of 1633. Old woodcut illustrations of plants are very good sources of ideas for foliated designs.*

LEFT: *Floral decorated initial from a missal, from around 1470.*

BELOW: *An initial letter from* The Roman de la Rose *at the beginning of the sixteenth century.*

on. Examine the different ways that leaves form on stems—are they opposite or alternate? Are the leaves palmately lobed like a maple, or are they palmately compound like a chestnut? Are the leaves themselves smooth-edged, toothed, or lobed? Are they oval, oblong, lance-shaped, or heart-shaped? All these different aspects of the plant form can give you ideas for a foliated pattern. If you understand these principles, you can then interpret the design in your own way. Remember that you are not trying to illustrate the plants. You are using them as the basis for an illuminated design. This usually means that the shapes you draw are simpler and probably more regular than would be found in nature.

Be restrained in your use of foliated designs. You could use a simple plant form for a terminal flourish or create a more complex pattern for a textural effect as part of an initial letter or to fill the counter shape.

89 *Foliated designs*

interlace and key patterns

With these patterns we return to where we began, with the early Dark Age illuminated manuscripts. One of the most attractive features of the decoration in these manuscripts, and the one that has inspired countless artists and designers throughout the centuries, is the use of interlace designs and key patterns. They were very much a part of the Celtic culture of Western Europe and were used not only in manuscripts but also on carved stone crosses, jewelry, and other artifacts. The various patterns have been given names such as fret, plait, and knot interlace.

ABOVE: *Simple interlace design.*

BELOW: *A basic element that forms the basis of a more complex knot interlace design.*

RIGHT: *Complex interlace and foliated designs on a cross in Campbeltown, Argyll, Scotland (White's Archaeological Sketches in Scotland, 1873).*

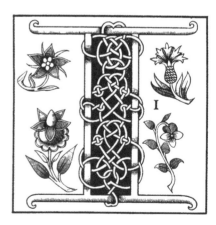

ABOVE: *Illuminated letter 'I' from* Cramer's Bible, 1539.

Part three—Exercises and projects

Drawing these designs is one of the greatest challenges you will encounter in illumination. They can be extremely complex. It is best to begin by tracing many different examples before you embark on your own designs. If you have a rule and compass, use these tools to draw the straight lines and curves. Start with some simple straight-line patterns, both interlace and key designs, with just a few repeats. Gradually increase the complexity of the designs. Patterns with curves will be more difficult to draw accurately. Finally, add some color and gold.

Study illustrations of old manuscripts and note how and where interlace and key patterns have been used, both as part of the lettering and as decoration. As with all the other aspects of illuminated lettering described in this book, remember that once you have understood the principles of the craft, you can develop your own ideas rather than restrict yourself to those of the past. We live in the twenty-first century!

ABOVE: *Illustration from Russian 15th century gospel "of Volkovyskoye."*

LEFT: *Calligraphy from a 13th century Novgorod gospel.*

References

GLOSSARY

ascender The stroke of lowercase letters that rises above the x-height (as in b, d, and h).

bestiary A medieval book form of a moral nature on beasts.

book hand A style of handwritten lettering used for the main text of books.

broad-edge pen A pen with a writing tip that has a chisel-shape end; also square-edge pen.

burnisher A smooth-tipped tool used for polishing.

calligraphy Writing as an art, beautiful writing, penmanship.

capitals The initial, or "large," letters of an alphabet.

centered Text or image placed at an equal distance from the left and right margins.

counter The space contained within round parts of letters.

cursive Flowing handwriting or calligraphy.

descender The part of lowercase letters (such as g, y, and q) that lies below the baseline.

entasis A central narrowing of the thickness of a line or object (e.g., the vertical stoke of a letter "I" or a column of a building).

flourish A (nonessential) embellishment added to a letter.

gesso A compound based on plaster of Paris or gypsum used as a ground for painting or on which to apply gold in illumination.

gold leaf Real gold beaten or pressed to a very thin sheet.

ground See gesso.

gum arabic A water-based glue.

herbal A book with descriptions of herbs and plants.

incipit pages The introductory pages that introduce chapters in early manuscripts. These are usually richly illuminated.

Indian ink A black pigment made from charcoal.

italic A style of cursive calligraphy and writing developed in Italy during the Renaissance. Also a slanting version of a typeface, sometimes of a slightly different and more cursive style.

justified text A block of text that has straight right and left margins.

letter spacing The space between letters. This is different from the physical distance between letters.

ligature Two or more letters joined together to make a single alphabetic symbol.

line space The space between lines of text.

lowercase The "small" letters of the alphabet (abcdefg, etc.).

margin The white spaces around text blocks.

medium (plural media) The process or material used to create art works or designs.

nib width The width of the writing end of a broad-edge pen.

papyrus A material used by early cultures for writing, made from the papyrus reed.

parchment A writing material made from animal skin, including calf (as vellum), sheep, goat, and even human.

pen angle The angle the writing tip of the broad-edge pen makes with the horizontal writing line.

PVA Polyvinyl acetate, a chemical compound made into a white water-soluble adhesive.

raised gilding A technique used in illumination, in which the gold leaf is applied to a raised gesso ground.

reservoir The small, metal attachment on a pen nib, which helps to control the flow of ink.

scriptorium The room in which the medieval scribes wrote their manuscripts and taught other scribes.

serif The strokes at the end of a letter's main strokes.

slope The angle that the vertical lines of letters make with the horizontal writing line.

style The character of a letterform.

texture In the physical sense, the quality of a surface. Texture can also be visual.

typography The use of typefaces in designs.

uncials An early form of writing that lacks capitals and which was developed from the Roman scripts.

unjustified Text that has a straight right or left margin with the opposite margin uneven (ragged).

vellum A writing material made from calfskin, widely used by Dark Age and Medieval scribes.

word spacing The distance between words in text.

x-height The height of the lowercase letter x.

BIBLIOGRAPHY

Alexander, Jonathan J. G., *Medieval Illuminators and Their Methods of Work*, Yale University Press, 1992

Backhouse, Janet, *The Illuminated Manuscript*, Phaidon Press, 1979

Cirker, Blanche, *The Book of Kells*, Dover, 1982

De Hamel, Christopher, *A History of Illuminated Manuscripts*, Phaidon Press, 1994

De Hamel, Christopher, *The British Library Guide to Manuscript Illumination: History and Technique*, University of Toronto Press, 2002

Drogan, Marc, *Medieval Calligraphy: Its History and Technique*, Dover, 1989

Grafton, Carol Belanger (editor), *Illuminated Initials in Full Colour: 548 Designs*, Dover, 1995

Johnston, Edward, *Writing and Illuminating and Lettering*, Dover, 1995

Lovett, Patricia, *Calligraphy and Illumination: A History and Practical Guide*, Harry N Abrams, 2000

Marmion, Simon and Thorpe, James, *Books of Hours: Illuminations*, H. E. Huntington Library and Art, 2003

Whitley, Kathleen P., *The Gilded Page: The History and Technique of Manuscript Gilding*, Oak Knoll Books, 2000

WEB SITES

http://www.leavesofgold.org/
Leaves of Gold. Treasures of manuscript illumination from Philadelphia collections.

http://www.kb.nl/kb/manuscripts/
Medieval illuminated manuscripts.

http://www.metmuseum.org/toah/hd/iman/hd_iman.htm
Manuscript illumination in Italy (1400–1600 A.D.).

http://www.medievalarthistory.com/manuscripts.html
Illumination (links to a number of sites on the subject of calligraphy and illumination).

INDEX

ACKNOWLEDGMENTS

Acknowledgment is due to several people who contributed to this book.

Special thanks go to Maureen Sullivan for the text and illustrations for projects one, two, and three and to Janet Mehigan for project four. Dave Wood and Donald Jackson kindly gave their permission to reproduce their innovative calligraphy (*page 15*). I also thank Rebecca Saraceno for so seamlessly and painlessly guiding the work through the editorial process.

Permission was granted to reproduce illustrations from illuminated manuscripts by the following libraries and institutions:

Bridgeman Art Library:
pp. 6, 10, British Library, London; 8, Winchester Cathedral, Hampshire; 9, Collection, Earl Leicester, Holkham Hall, Norfolk; 11, Board Trinity College, Dublin; 13L, 37T, Bibliotheque Mazarine, Paris; 13R, Topham Picturepoint.

The **ILLUMINATED LETTERING KIT**

Usus est magister optimus.